Brushstrokes

Also by Jill Gloyne
The Slip-rails are Down (with Bev Willson),
Kookaburra Press, 1992
You just had to deal with it, Hyde Park Press, 1997
The Nautilus Shell...and other tales, Hyde Park Press, 1999
New Poets Nine, Wakefield Press, 2004

Jill Gloyne

Brushstrokes

Acknowledgements

The following poems have been previously published:
'The Crab': *Friendly Street Poets* 30, 2006
'Croix de La Rochette': *Rewired, Friendly Street Poets* 32, 2008
'North Terrace, Adelaide': *Unruly Sun, Friendly Street Poets* 31, 2007
'Springtime in Melbourne': *Five Bells*, Vol. 15, No. 1,
Summer 2007–2008
'Fishing at Chapman River': *Five Bells*, Vol. 9, No. 1, Summer 2002
'I am Orange': Poem of the Month, Friendly Street Poets, 2006
'Lost': *Weekend Australian*, March 6–7, 2004
'Rehearsal': *Southern Write*, September 2012
'Insomnia': *Australian Poetry Ltd Members Anthology*, 2012
'Villanelle': *Central Coast Poets Inc.*, 2000
'Song Without Words': *Kingfisher Collection*,
Karrinyup Writers' Club Inc., 2003
'Alphabet': *Blue Dog: Australian Poetry*, Vol. 16, No. 11
'Lady Macbeth': *Blur, Friendly Street Poets* 29, 2005
'Scar': *Wet Ink*, Issue 13, December 2008
'Eating Figs': Poem of the Month, Friendly Street Poets, 2008
'Parting with a Friend': *Blur, Friendly Street Poets* 29, 2005
'Enigma': *A Poetry Anthology*, Central Coast Poets, 2002

The following poems have won awards:
'Making Bread': Winner of the inaugural
Martha Richardson Award, 2003
'Pruning the Vine': Winner of the
Wannabee Publishing Poetry Competition, 2003
'Plus ça Change': Winner of the
Wannabee Publishing Poetry Competition, 2004

Brushstrokes
ISBN 978 1 76041 278 4
Copyright © text Jill Gloyne 2017
Cover image: © Scott Hartshorne 2017, used with permission

First published 2016 by
GINNINDERRA PRESS
PO Box 3461 Port Adelaide 5015 Australia
www.ginninderrapress.com.au

Contents

First Words	9
Poets	10
What is Poetry?	11
Song Without Words	12
It's Just Semantic	13
Plus ça Change	14
Etymology	15
Wordsmith	16
Solitaire	17
Head Over Heels	18
Cinderella	19
Honey	21
Poetry Editor	22
Alphabet	23
Geometrics	32
Shakespeare's Toolbox	33
Let's Not Compare	34
Lady Macbeth	35
Destiny	36
Scar	37
My Son, My Son	38
Footprints in the Sand	39
Sisyphus	40
Diamond Mine	41
A Rose is a Rose	42
Just a Piece of Furniture	43
Strings	48
Shadow Play	49
Broken Lines	50
Knots	52

From A to U	53
Gift	54
Coup de Téléphone	55
Haiku for Lease	56
Links	57
Every Face a Different Mask	58
Bonsai	63
Verandas	64
Ghosts of Walloway Plain	65
Drought	66
Symphony	67
Ghost of Dead Horse Creek	68
Curdimurka Ball	69
Flinders Ranges	70
Wood Turner	71
Dance for me Jack	72
Fridge Magnet	73
Mr Thursday	74
Millie Dear	77
Churinga	79
For Hilda	80
Making Bread	81
Apricots	82
Eating Figs	83
Sunday Lunch	84
Parting With a Friend	85
The Crab	86
Croix de La Rochette	87
Good Friday	88
Spring-cleaning	89
North Terrace, Adelaide	90
Springtime in Melbourne	91

Ward Round, 1952	92
Order in the House	93
Ypres, Belgium, 1950	94
Soldier Settler	96
After the War	97
Arms Dealer	98
Suspect	99
But for the Grace	100
Enigma	101
Coming Home in Spring	102
Evensong	103
Reveille	104
Road Kill	105
Fishing at Chapman River	106
Paper Nautilus	108
New Year's Eve	109
July in Penneshaw	111
Sea Song	112
Snug Cove, Kangaroo Island	113
Treading Grapes	114
Villanelle	115
I am Orange	116
Golden Wedding	117
Pruning the Vine	118
Dried Figs	119
In the Shadow of Each Other's Presence	120
Lost	121
Rehearsal	122
Maxie	123
Cliff Edge	124
Wreckage	125
Death is Never Convenient	126

Insomnia	127
Alone	128
Love Letters	129
Orpheus and Eurydice	130
Last Words	131

First Words

My mother fed me my first words.
Entranced, I asked for more.
As toys and tools, words led me to another world.
At night, door shut against loneliness,
I practised different combinations,
fabricated friends who talked all night
until, exhausted, we packed away our syntax
and slept in a smile slung between two brackets.
Books read me as I read them.
I travelled the world in a dictionary
hand in hand so I would not get lost.
A thesaurus arrived, slept under my pillow
to deepen the coloured layers of my dreams.

Those first few words my mother fed me
feed me still. And I am just as hungry.

Poets

They come in all shapes and sizes
like antique bottles and jars:
short and squat, square or round,
blue and green and brown
or with a glass ball in the neck
to hold in effervescence,
defence against explosions
that might shatter them.

I have found them hidden in closets,
among ruins of old buildings,
on rubbish dumps, at garage sales
and under old Akubras.
They have no labels to tell you
who or what they are or were,
but if you rub them gently,
very gently,
a genie might emerge.

What is Poetry?

What is poetry? she asked.
Ah, poetry, I sighed
into the waiting wind.

Poetry is what you do not say
with words you do not write.
Hidden in an image
it leaps from the page,
draws blood and
gives succour to the soul.

Song Without Words

He was a simple man. Unversed. Or worse.
Illiterate. Barely articulate. Tripped over words
like stumbling blocks. Misread their meaning,
leaning as they did at awkward angles
in their sentence. Preferred to disentangle
fencing wire and fishing line,
not convoluted letters of the mind.

And yet, between his workman's hands there grew
a wordless song that flew each time he looked upon his life,
his wife. His eyes to hers wrote poetry he knew
she understood. No need for metre, assonance or rhyme.
No cause to write, recite, communicate by mail.
At night his fingers traced unwritten lines,
translating, as he went, his text to Braille.

It's Just Semantic

I couldn't, wouldn't, shouldn't
be your lover.
You shouldn't, couldn't, wouldn't
be mine.
      So why all the fuss,
as if we have, when we haven't
done what we didn't
because we can't.
The won't, the shan't
do not apply in
love's linguistics.
We both know
we would if we could.

Plus ça Change

Cinderella's liberated now:
Domestic Science teacher, permanent
position, sick pay, holidays and even, wow!
a place on the Board of Education, meant,

of course, as a sop to gender bias, yet
nevertheless, a step in the right direction
upwards, where the hard dark glass reflects
the ceiling of her feminist ambition,

an atrium of opportunity.
After school, collects the kids, delivers
them to tennis, football, junior hockey,
music, ballet, just as if she were

a lackey. Heats takeaways in microwaves
(nutrition's left the school curriculum)
and Sunday is the day she tries to save
for quality of time as well as cleaning.

Drives a Volvo, pumpkin-coloured, over-
drafted into service, constantly
exhausted at the midnight hour, like her.
At night, too tired for sex, and so is he,

she falls upon the bed in fitful sleep,
sees before her slippers, row on row,
and princes, all so charming she could weep
that she's no longer Cinderella, knows
that though she's been so busy swapping glass,
she's still caught in the same age-old impasse.

Etymology

Nominative, genitive,
accusative, dative,
all as silent
as a dying tongue.

Their case has been dismissed.
Glitz and glamour have gone from grammar
and spelling staggers under the hammer
of the phonetically inclined.

But I need words to live,
spell out their history.
I am defined by language.
Each word I use
tells me who I am.

Wordsmith

For the time being
I am serving a sentence
in solitary confinement.
My cell is empty,
except for the alphabet.
I create words, sentences,
turn them into poems,
novels, reports, histories.
I translate them into
another language, then another.
I employ the entire world
in communication.
I fill every library, bookshelf
and school bag that ever was.
What's more, I do all this
with twenty-six solitary letters.

Solitaire

Shuffle
deal
then play
with patience.

Try to find
the card you need.

Repeat

and repeat
once more
until

the cards fall into place
like words
looking for a poem.

Head Over Heels

She wanted to write a poem so she went for a walk in the woods to pick a bunch of flowers which she placed end to end in a long sentence that wandered on and on forever and ever Amen.

When she held it up to the light
it fluttered in the breeze like a silk ribbon.
That is a beautiful thought, she said,
and cut it into short lengths,
placing them on the page,
one after the other
in the right order
very neatly.
Then she signed it.

When he walked past
he stopped and read her poem.
Without a word
he picked up the scissors,
cut out the lines
and turned them upside down.

Before she could turn away
he gave her his eyes
so she could read it.
Ah! she smiled,
handing them back.
I see.

Cinderella

How was I to know he was a cross-dresser?
You'd think his satin pants were good enough,
baby blue, skin tight, *très* sexy, with
frilled lace and real diamonds on his shoes.
But no. He wants to drown
in Milady's gowns.
Some nights he goes through
my entire wardrobe.
And as for those glass slippers –
clippety-clop, clippety-clop –
upstairs, downstairs,
in my lady's chamber,
all through the palace like
a horse with a limp.

Worst of all, though, is the betrayal.
You know, him and my fairy godmother.
That bitch. The witch. Or is she, I wonder,
under all that hocus pocus,
a wizard in drag? Either way,
he simply cannot leave her fairy wand alone.
Every night it's, 'Let's do the pumpkin bit again.'
And off they go, cavorting around the town
like Emma Bovary, waving a Kleenex
from the window of the carriage.

But tonight, I got my revenge.
Oh, you should have seen their faces.
I offered to do dinner for them both;
after all, Cinders is no stranger to Downstairs.
Five gourmet courses with vintage wines.
They loved it, they said, simply divine,
but did I get any thanks? You're kidding.
Not a word. Just, 'Let's do the pumpkin bit',
and off they went as usual.
Of course, I knew they'd be back.
'Seen our pumpkin anywhere downstairs?'
they asked. I picked up my knitting
and made them wait while I counted the stitches –
it was a very complicated pattern –
'Why yes, guys,' I replied eventually.
'You've just had it.'

Honey

Life is like honey, dripping on thorns,
soothing and smoothing, a poem soft told,
healing the wounds to which we were born.

With heartache and injury, bleeding and torn,
reach for the humming hive's rich, golden glow.
Life is like honey, dripping on thorns.

Without the scars of His rough crown of thorns
Christ could not give us His promise foretold:
the healing of wounds to which we are born.

Darkness and death we need no longer mourn,
for death is not final, its sting can't withhold
a life that is honey, dripping on thorns.

Life gives us joy, and to joy we're reborn
when the warmth and aroma of flowers unfold
healing the wounds to which we are born.

So savour the honey, the balm of the swarm
look into its mirror yourself to behold
healing the wounds to which we are born
life is pure honey dripping on thorns.

Poetry Editor

Or: On the Demise of the Definite Article

Like a man with a fetish,
through poem after poem,
he ferrets them out:
ubiquitous culprits
that hide behind nouns
like recalcitrant adjectives
on every line.

'Out, out!' he screams
fanatically,
brandishing his red biro
with cutting precision.

Like soldiers,
battle-scarred and weary,
they stagger, shame-faced,
to their Waterloo
and disappear,
to be eclipsed by syntax
or perhaps,
even
saved by poetic licence.

Alphabet

A

Wouldn't you think that Icarus,
if he needed a brighter globe,
would proceed with caution
up that ladder
and heed the warning;
Do not climb above this step.
But oh no, not him.
One step too far and then
that spectacular crash-landing.

B

Bottoms like to dance cheek to cheek.
That's why they come in pairs.

C

Do you think the moon
is really made of cheese:
that every month
the heat of passion
melts its edges,
strand by sticky strand,
until it disappears
into the single string of a hammock?

If you do,
come milk the cow with me.

D

Your tiny feet beat tattoos
on the taught drum of my belly,
announce the next performance
in this bright silk circus tent.

Inside, the trapeze artist knows
he has an inbuilt safety net,
but I know
he cannot take it with him.

E

Turn each dead end into a runway
and take off with the birds.
Weave the thread of your sentence
into the ribbon of sky,
tie it to the wind
and let it fly.

F

We don't use gibbets any more,
or Mediaeval torture.
We have refined the system
based on the fact we all
take a life to die.

G

Your mind is curling into
the foetus it once was.
I see you every day in the park,
hunched over a memory
that has faded into
the shrinking horizon
of a vacant stare.

Your mind is taking
your body with it.

H

Why hold me at arm's length?
Why not drop the bar
so we can stand together,
become an L?
Love starts with L.

I said L, not Hell.

I

When I look in the mirror
I see the loneliest letter
in the alphabet.

J

Gentle hooks reach out
from the corners of your eyes,
hold me firm
in the strength of your smile.

K

Don't tell me,
let me guess:
you went to the fancy dress ball
as a wind turbine?

A three-masted schooner!

Well,
you should have given
the drink a miss.

L

Corners are good
for hiding things,
leaning into
or joining lonely lines.

But going round them can be dangerous.

I once turned the heel of a sock
and nearly lost my soul.

M

To bite into the silhouette of night
moon blades sharpen jagged teeth
in metal jaws outside the tractor shed.

N

Life is either
a very steep climb
or a slippery slide.

Just ask Sisyphus.

O

Alpha and Omega:
it starts where
it ends where
it starts where

it swallows its tail
like Ourobouros.

Of course,
as a number,
it becomes zero,
nothing,

an orifice to disappear
into
forever.

P

I'm tired of feeding you
three times a day,
playing 'post the letter'
just to get you to eat
what I take ages to prepare.

When you feed yourself,
I'll paint your high chair
pillar box red and buy you
a baseball cap with
Australia Post on the front.

Q

Some people do not like cats.
They decapitate them.

R

R you, R you really
such a preposterous shape,
striding into the future
with that swollen head?

Or are you dragging yourself
back to the past with a
lump humped on your back,
a chip upon your shoulder?

S

Love is never straight forward.
It is the transparent skin
shed from the twists and turns of life.

T

The problem with a T-junction is
you have to make a choice.

U

Hug yourself if you must,
you with the big round bottom;
make yourself slim at the top,
but remember,
when you're middle-aged
everything goes pear-shaped.

V

Temptation's cleavage, fertile ground
for all that makes the world go round.
Where, oh where, would the novel be
without that central letter V?

W

Once upon a time
the garbage truck's forks
inadvertently scooped me up,
tossed me into the back
and ground me into compost
for the council to sell.

The neighbours thought
I'd left my husband,
moved interstate to a better job,
whatever;

they have no idea I am reclining
in their garden pushing up
the odd daisy.

X

They stand side by side at the altar.
Later they will join together
in an act pivotal to their union,
a cross to bear or revere.

But for now their signatures
are an unknown quantity.

Y

If your neckline
plunges any deeper,
it will become
the why I want you.

Z

You think you're a cartoonist's dream,
snoozing as you do,
in all those thought balloons.

But when you link into the zigzag
of a lightning strike
that dream becomes a nightmare.

Geometrics

I
know
that in a poem
all parallel lines meet in
truth, taking me to another sphere
where I can fly in a vast circumference
unencumbered by regulations, aware there is no
pi to quantify its ratio to me. Sometimes I become a
reactionary rhomboid whose angles will not add up to 360
degrees, whose solutions do not produce a QED, and
whose many interpretations never translate into
the language that surrounds me. Shapes
of various dimensions create their
own sweet, honeyed tongue. So
what if I choose my own
and fly to the moon
on a beam
now
?

Shakespeare's Toolbox

When Shakespeare was a little boy he was given a toolbox. It was made of old English oak. Inside he discovered twenty-six wooden tools, each one carved in a different shape. He loved them so much he played with them all day. At night he stood them on the mantelpiece so he could see them before he went to sleep and as soon as he awoke in the morning. He made them into words which he used like bricks to build walls of sentences joined by the mortar of his thoughts. Before long they covered the entire floor. He knew they were better than his friends' train sets. His sentences could leave their tracks and fly to a world where anything could happen and often did.

When he fell in love he built a wall around his heart. It was fourteen rows high and ten bricks wide. He checked the stress of each row with a pentameter and made sure they ended in harmony with each other. He liked it so much he built some more.

He entertained his friends in a globe where actors tossed his words back and forth with the thrust and parry of brilliant repartee. The audience applauded so much they forced his stories up through the open roof where they hung like curtains in the clouds above. Even after four hundred years they still feed us whenever it rains.

His tools have never worn out.

Let's Not Compare

If you expect to read an English sonnet,
think again. Who wants to read iambic
pentameter today? Who gets their kicks
from fourteen lines, three stanzas and a couplet,
or has the time for regimented verse
demanding as it does so strict a rhyme,
a b a b and so on down the line
or abba which I know is even worse?
Poor Shakespeare wrote one hundred fifty-four,
the lovesick coot. Was that the only way
that he could get a satisfactory lay,
to write all day and then rewrite some more?
Today, amongst his fans, he'd have a ball;
with verse as free as love, he'd fuck them all.

Lady Macbeth

She was never very good
at knitting without a pattern –
and now she's lost it.

Her problem lies between
the stitch she dropped and guilt
at having to unravel a sleeve
that will not be cast off.

Her grand design has tied her
into knots she can't undo
to wash away the stain
of blood-red needles.

Sweet sleep, for her, will never
die a natural death again.

Destiny

I
I knew
I knew you
I knew you would
I knew you would die
I knew you would die young.

You
You could
You could not
You could not see
You could not see it
You could not see it coming.

We
We cannot
We cannot change
We cannot change things
We cannot change things around
We cannot change things around us.

Scar

We were so poor I had to compromise on every thought.
If I expected food for a meal I might have to settle for a
memory of it until I could eat no more.

If I was shivering from cold I would have to seek out
some warm colour to wrap around my mind, very tightly,
until I stopped trembling.

I survived in this not-have world by learning to stitch
together the rough edges of sorrow with a silken hair from
my grandmother; she taught invisible mending.

My Son, My Son

When you first took him in your arms
a world of warmth and wonder
hung, like gold dust,
in the air around you.
You could not wait to
start your dedication of love.
Words were your vocation.

You did not know that one day in the future
those words would catch in your throat,
pulled taught by the noose of a question mark
hanging, unanswered, at the end of a line,
your cry echoing down the years:
'Oh Absolom, my son, my son.'

Footprints in the Sand

At night, those screeching tyres
skid through my head again,
leaving the smell of rubber
burning in my brain.

I wish the tide would wash away
this debris from my mind,
leaving me a brand-new page
my story to rewind.

Oh, how I long to walk along
that pure and pristine strand
and see, instead of wheel tracks,
my own footprints in the sand.

Sisyphus

You say a child was put to death
in this, the cradle of a mind,

not violently, by harsh intent,
with sword of fire or twisted cord

but slowly down the ladder of her years
with thoughtless blows that wrenched away

the rungs she needed for support
to reach the longed-for heights

she rarely saw. Each time she fell
she rose again, with barbs to push her on

climbing that weary road alone
each step a cutting plea to glimpse

her bright imagined goal before
she tripped and slowly fell once more.

Diamond Mine

Today I saw where you were born
wrenched from an inflexible rock;

not an easy birth, yet you shine
like a supernova.

Alone, aloof,
you do not share your passion,

explode with radiance like liquid opal
or weep, like a pearl, from the heart.

Dry-eyed, detached and proudly regal,
you float in a sea of frozen flame,

an iceberg bearing hidden danger
below your cool, hard surface.

Your brilliance burns like fire. I know.
I have the scars to prove it.

A Rose is a Rose

With apologies to Gertrude Stein

You seduced me with a single rose
and a lingering kiss. I had never known
such bliss. I was on fire.

Drunk on the perfume of desire
I did not heed the call:
                'Be warned!
A rose by any name adorned
hides deadly thorns below each bud
draws blood-red tears of grief, not love.'

A lie is a lie, is a lie.

Just a Piece of Furniture

i

That's right. Sit on me,
like you always do. Just think
of your comfort, not of mine.
I do have feelings you know.
Jealousy rips me apart
each time you take cushions
from that smart settee to hide
my worn out contours.
Besides, their brilliance
overpowers my shabbiness.
It's cruel to criticise
what you neglect;
a bright new outfit
could so easily uplift me.

Just wait. I'm working
on a broken spring.
That should fix you.

ii

At last. I thought
you'd never come to bed.
Yes, I know I'm comfortable,
orthopaedically designed,
a spring in every step.
Two hundred and six
individual pieces
exquisitely articulated
take your weight upon me
night after horizontal night.

iii

You think
you've got me framed
but you're framed too.
I've got you covered
every time you pass me by.
Admit it. You need me
to see yourself
as others do.
Without me
you would not exist.

iv

I'm not, by nature, frigid;
just rigidly controlled.
Even though I lose my cool
each time you reach inside,
that, too, is control of a kind.

Were I to melt into your warmth
I'd start to propagate the rot
that I'm supposed to stop.
But that can't be. Our fate's decreed.

v

So, you can read me like a book.
Not surprising, considering
you've got me up against the wall.

Tell me, am I fact or fiction?
I need your help.
I do not know myself.

vi

Whatever you do
don't open me.
Darkness hides the
distance between us,
keeping your face
as it used to be.
I could paint it
from memory,
blindfolded.

Yes, I know
the drawstring works
but please, don't touch,
leave it as it is.
The blinding light
might change
our world forever.

vii

Last night
I didn't hear you pack your things
I didn't hear you tell me why
I didn't hear you.

This morning
I'm stripped bare of all
but hollow echoes,
empty hangers tremble
in their vacancy.

I cannot find my clothes.

Strings

When you hooked up my skirt
to manipulate my movements,
did you think you could control me,
just like that, parting my legs
with your silken threads?

You made me sing and dance,
your fingers a question mark
under my skin, but did you think
my steps would follows yours
voluntarily?

I am no puppet mouthing
someone else's thoughts.
I sing my own song,
dance to my own tune,
no strings attached.

Shadow Play

The day you lost your shadow
gathering clouds blocked out the sun.

Did you lose it accidentally
or was it by design?

When I found it hanging like a halo
you struck me to the ground with angry blows

and would not take it back.
Yet still it hung, unbidden.

Now you pass with leaden steps
preceded by that elongated shape,

a weight so burdensome it seems
there is no lighter life for dreams.

Broken Lines

i

Our love
was once a gold balloon
floating towards the sun.

But now it's ripped
to strips of rubber,
a ricochet of tension
pulled back and forth
across the kitchen table.

Finally, worn out,
it snapped,
a stinging blow.

Over-stretched
it cannot be rejoined.

ii

The note
on the fridge
was brief:
'I've left.'

But those seven letters
hid a lengthy sentence
that pushed them so far apart
they could no longer
recognise each other.

iii

The flowers you never bought me
linger on. A splash of soursob yellow
spilling from a vase of faded tears.

Knots

Did you not understand
the Yin and Yang of ropes,
that lovers' knots,
though sewn askew,
are still a lover's knot,
and more forgiving
than the reef?

Each time you tried
to pull me close,
the knot grew tighter,
a tourniquet that
could not be released.

But if you'd used a slip knot,
with a loop at the end,
each time I fell
I could have found
my own way back
to you.

From A to U

The problem with our friendship,
she said, is the middle vowel.
You did not treat it with due care.
And when you swapped it for another
Plato's pleasant harmony
turned into Pluto's deep despair.

Gift

You gave me
part of yourself,
held out,
like a child's treasure,
on a grubby palm.
I blinked
to see more clearly,
but as I did
it blew away.

By the time
I found it again
you had tied it
so tightly
I could feel it
broken inside.

Coup de Téléphone

The telephone is not the place, the space, for this.
I need to see your eye, the why the lie. I miss
your smiling face, our laughing games.
If you had kept our rendezvous, you
might have felt me soothe your pain, again,
with touch, such as we used to do.
But now we talk through air where there
are no familiar words to share,
just those that tear, ensnare.
I'm lost. The cost of love without the trust
is much too high, so try,
when I hang up, as hang I must,
to understand it's more than just
a see-you-soon goodbye.

Haiku for Lease

This corner block
is not a living part
of the city.

Cyclone fencing sags
like the workers
trudging by.

Dull graffiti spews
frustration and resentment
onto speechless walls.

Daily papers
pile up in corners,
faded, trapped.

But angled correctly,
broken bottles might
fire their news

into burning
'expressions of
interest'.

Links

Grey ribbons of road
curl round the country

telegraph wires
sag with the weight of words

musical sails
ply the sea's full orchestra

vapour trails of biros
start in someone's hand
and finish in another's

twin railway lines
of thoughts
cross over

ends held together
by links that divide.

Every Face a Different Mask

i

Each day
the ritual never varies:
half an hour
to realign the face
her audience will see.

An act, made up.

ii

The only thing
that holds him together,
stops him falling apart
at the seams of his
baggy clown's trousers,
is the smile drawn on his face:
a smile, in greasepaint,
impervious to tears.

iii

Throughout the year
they argued every day;
bitched and bickered,
nagged and needled,
a continuous battle
of thrust and parry.
Their words,
barbed and sharp,
targeted open wounds,
tore them apart.

But once a year,
they put aside
their ammunition,
and threw a party.
Champagne, caviar,
you know, the works;
invited all to come and share
their wedding anniversary!

iv

She wishes the Yellow Brick Road
to Colton Ward
was make believe,
like the games she played
when she was little;

that postural drainage
was galloping horses,
and cystic fibrosis
was sixty-five roses.

And when she says,
'I'll get my lung function
back above 80, I will
you know,' she believes it.

She must. For years
she's breathed
the sterile air of nebulisers,
her smile held in place
by the hooks of medical research
she dare not remove.

v

The hand that serves
the sacred host, the Holy Ghost,
the Lord, the congregation,
little children,

can no longer hide
behind an upright collar,
under cassocks
or in a dark confessional.

The cross
has been debased.

vi

He worked frenetically
to fabricate respectability:

church warden (never missed a service),
chairman of the hospital board,
president of the school council,
secretary of the National Trust,
treasurer of the footy club.
He attended all these meetings
with regularity and punctuality
like a trained dog.
Nothing was too much trouble.
His generous donations
to popular causes
echoed across the community,
and his business prospered
with the usual signs of success.

But out of sight,
his wife wore bruises
with the humiliation
of a discarded coat,
found in the bottom of a Salvo's bin,
ill-fitting, in need of repair.

Bonsai

Like the pots he tended with such care
he bonsaied himself into a narrow thought
he would not feed for fear that it might grow.

His roots, gnarled for lack of space,
snarled at each other
like cars in a traffic jam. Above,
a mirror image of arms grew short,
too rigid to bend with the wind.

In all the years I knew him
he never grew.

The Botanical Gardens in Montreal
have a bonsai that's 500 years old.
It just won't die.
But then, it's barely lived.

Verandas

Like the drooping brim
of an old Akubra,
verandas shield us
from the glare
of our existence,
give us shelter
so we can safely
weather storms.

From birth to death
lives are played out
on these boards;
identities are found,
virginities lost
and deals are sealed
with the handshake
of a stubby.

Old furniture moves
from inside out,
broken springs
lie in wait for
unsuspecting bottoms,
sleeping louvres
enclose one end
with rusting snores,

and every month
the seasons hang
their pictures on its trellis,
a still life looking in
upon itself.

Ghosts of Walloway Plain

My childhood ghosts
are draped in mantles of dust;
fingers tap on the broken frame
of distant memories –
dead bones wanting in.

These ghosts have buried
so much time in drought
that only a song of Braille
can feel what's underneath
their shifting hands of sand.

Years ago they
tilled the soil with hope
but now, their lives long gone,
they howl to the sad-faced moon,
like dingoes wanting out.

This plain, demented
by the dregs of disillusion,
ribs the hot, dry wind
that flutes across its past,
a song that I find hard to grasp.

Drought

Like the seam of a shroud,
its stitches torn apart upon decay,
the road through Australia's heart
lays out its coat of arms
on either side.

The long paddock
is now a silent morgue.

In harsh metallic skies
the carrion call of crows
hangs like a windsock
in the still, dry air,
black armband
of morning, mourning.

Even the echo
is dead.

Symphony

For months we have waited for this.
It is an occasion to be savoured
by us all. The performance,
announced by rolling drums,
rains down in harmony.

Flutes trickle over parched memories,
violins fill our nostrils with sweet, damp earth,
cymbals crash with lightning speed
and music, overflowing
from strings to wind, bursts its banks.

Ecstatic, we rise to thunderous applause –
the first decent rain in years.

Ghost of Dead Horse Creek

Do your bones rise up
with the swooning sun
to dance with the jabiru

does your hand caress
her sensuous neck
of opalescent blue

do you wander both
through the watery reeds
just like you used to do

or lie upon
the grassy bank
washed by ghostly dew

and when the laser
lighted moon
sings songs for lovers true

do you dance I ask
do you dance I sing
do you dance with brolgas too?

Curdimurka Ball

Before

All day the ants are busy,
their hectic activity
a predetermined pattern
of construction.

When the fiery ball of sun
departs the day, grinning
through the broken teeth
of portaloos, all neat
and rigidly in line
along the rim that some great hand
has ruled across this empty page,
the ants are satisfied.

The stage is set.

After

The party's over.

Three thousand snores and farts
perpetuate the myth
that man is all hot air,
his thunderous activity
a mere blip in the dreamtime.

Next day, the ants are gone.

Flinders Ranges

Steeped in prayer and stooped in thought
these purple-cowled monks
file past in stately cortege
to a compline fixed in time.

They tell their beads in unison,
undercurrents of muffled prayer
that run through mountain ranges
with a rock-strong faith.

Anchored by the gravity of history
layer upon layer washes over them
in a sea of memory that erodes
a grain of sand each day.

They are a silent order.
But when the evening sunlight catches
ancient craggy heads,
all colour sings in deafening praise.

Wood Turner

See how they move in concert,
the curving timber and the man,
as songs from well-logged seasons
curl from the keening lathe.

So many revolutions
must be harnessed to unwind
the sedentary rhythms
from this ingrained burl of time.

He sets his tools and sees,
with his first glance, the finished bowl,
and with his last perceptive touch
releases to the world its hidden soul.

Dance for me Jack

for my grandson

Dance for me Jack
when I am gone,
dance for me
in your Blundstone boots.

With the beat of your feet
let the rhythm arise
like a vesper cloud
at the end of prayer.

Then I will wrap
in petals of silk
a gift soft tied
with angel's hair;

whenever
the spider orchids bloom
I'll dance for you
if you'll be there.

Fridge Magnet

Fingerprints of jam or Vegemite
adorn the fridge door,
impressionist impressions.
Walking across the white enamel,
more or less at the same level,
they could be the musical notation
of a heart that skips a beat,
a throat that catches every now and then
with the touch of a tiny hand
that reaches out and leaves behind
a sticky mess that firmly binds
the generation's span.

Mr Thursday

for my grandfather

Standing in the tunnel
of yesterday's century,
outlined by light
that splits the house in two
from door to door,

an old man hitches to his armpits
trousers from a taller son,
khaki remnant of Tobruk,
reflected glory,
worn each day with pride.

After school he welcomes us
with eyes that listen,
ears that see the need
to show us how to earn
what can't be bought.

In scorching heat his water bag
gives cool and sweet a crystal
purified by wrigglers in the tank,
their ballet dance a question mark
of undecided commas.

His voice enfolds us
like the smell of home-made bread,
leaven rising imperceptibly
in the childhood tales he tells.
In later years

through the lens of memory,
we focus on this wisdom
found amongst the mortar
crumbling from the cracks
between his words.

Shopkeepers in O'Connell Street
call him Mr Thursday;
like a well-oiled clock,
treasured for dependability,
his routine never varies.

The girl with peaches in her cheeks,
weighs out his fruit and veg
from a shopping list as neat
as invisible stitches
on worn elbows.

With string bags balancing his stride
he walks the scales of friendship
along the smile of the hour it takes
to pass one block of shops
and then another.

The spring in his step has sung
the song of the miles he's walked,
like a spontaneous chorus
reaching out to touch
more people than he knows

and like a well-pitched note,
echoing down the valley
of sharp recall,
his whistle summons
the ghosts of Thursday.

Millie Dear

My Gran
taught me to knit
on old bone needles
with wool handed down
like a genetic yarn.
She kept me on the straight and narrow
so Teddy's scarf would finish
with the same number of stitches
I had cast on.
From her I learnt that
knitting love into my patterns
would keep my dear ones warm
even when the jumper was threadbare.

Some nights
she liked to embroider
stars onto a parchment moon
so she could see herself
reflected in their exquisite creation.
As her eyesight failed
she used silken strands of memory
on her needle threader,
her stitches so neat and invisible
you could not see
where the past finished
or where the future
was about to begin.

Seated
at the easel of her world
she painted it in pastels;
not red and orange or shocking pink
but dusky rose, pale blue and lavender.
Oh, the scent of lavender bushes
that grew in her garden
and perfumed all our drawers
from sachets she made.
Even now, each time
I crush those flowers
in the palm of the hand she guided,
their aroma sings me to sleep.

Churinga

I am sitting in the kitchen at the table
cutting up vegetables for soup,
but I'm not cutting up vegetables
at the table where I am not sitting.
Someone else now owns this house.
They have modernised it;
brought the toilet inside
with their hygienic hands,
discarded friendly fireplaces
and the stove now uses
heat that can't be seen.
In fact they've dragged it,
struggling to remain itself,
into the twentieth century.
In spite of them, I still empty
the wash up bowl on the garden
(they call it grey water now)
and newspaper still heats
the water for my shower
with a roar that takes me back
to wooden bath mats, ice chests
and canvas water bags. My spirit
inhabits the soul of their house
but I do not disturb them.
They cannot see me. I belong
to a day when dawn walked down
the street with pint-sized steps,
leaving creamy milk in its wake
and yeast swelled with pride overnight.
But my heart still beats in time
to the chime of the hour on the wall
that held me in and let me out.

For Hilda

Each year you moved
like some instinctive animal
seeking hibernation
in the removalist's van.

Amazingly
the furniture survived;
with stoic resignation
scratches turned to face the wall
as if this misdemeanour was their fault,
bookshelves
wreathed in smiling words
covered broken wounds
and curtains
lengthened with a faded fringe
the colour of reeds
bound the depths of your feelings
to a solid bank.

The gardens
always greeted you
as if with expectation
smiling at the colour of your touch
and every home
was painted with your welcome.

Making Bread

Sunlight, on its winter bias, scarves
her hair with bands of silver. Floured hands,
in ritual creation, sculpt the heart
of the world from a grain of wheat. Sand

metes out the time she needs to work her dough,
knuckling invisible points of air, again
and again, with expertise, to and fro,
back and forth, until it's ready. Then

dividing it, she rolls out strips, plaits
them like her daughter's hair, the final glaze,
a smile from the yolk of the sun, a song that's
set to sing with the voice of warming rays.

She does not set the world on fire to prove
her worth. Proves it daily beside her stove.

Apricots

Just look at the apricot tree this year,
all those golden orbs lying in the
lap of the sun, soaking up its warmth.
See how, when I reach out
to touch the sunset of their day,
they blush, coy and seductive,
pleading to be plucked.

I will. Your flesh will simmer
till perfume webs
each corner of the house
with smiles of satisfaction.
For we know
when winter comes,
each time we open up a jar
your summer sun will fill the room.

Eating Figs

We came upon the ruins of a house
huddled beside a pepper tree and a fig,
the bitter-sweet of dour survival.
A late sun angled memories
through the canopy above,
lashing shadows against the wall,
silent echoes of a wrecker's ball.

The ground for miles around was bare,
barren as the mortar of hope
that all those distant years ago
was mixed too weak and dry
to bind these stones together
for a lifetime. Only the trees
had lived to reach old age.

The figs were bursting open,
sweet and succulent.
We let their juices mix with ours
until the budding mortar of our hope
took up new strength
and sent us on our way.

Sunday Lunch

Carved by a generation of homework,
like a resurfaced Pompeii, the table
on the veranda is our meeting place.
As we gather for our meal, sunlight drips
through vines on the nearby trellis,
glazing us with amber oil, a warming glow
distilled from leaves of our family tree.
Unspoken rituals simmer down the centuries:
mannerisms, recipes, the way we garden,
clean the house – because we've always done it so.
We pick the bones of history, sweet and succulent,
secure in the knowledge of who we are.
Year after year our children add their own spice
to flavour future gatherings under the vines, different,
yet surprisingly like those which went before.

Parting With a Friend

for Graziella

Who would have thought the border
between two countries would lie in
a suburban fence on common ground
where we would meet; that you

would take my Celtic cloak, paint it
with colours from the Adriatic Sea
and partner me with music
when I dance on Cornish moors.

Day by day we weave
enduring patterns with our threads,
your weft my warp together,
made firmer by the shuttle

of our passage back and forth
through friendship's gateway,
whose hinge, like a horizon,
holds us fast.

But now it's time to say goodbye,
so you take the earth and I'll take the sky.

The Crab

For years I've watched
that sideways scramble to the sea,
as if bias gave protection
from the crashing waves.
I wish.

They talk of chemotherapy;
it's not a sentence,
just a word, they say.
But can the doctors read
your star sign's hieroglyphics?

Now we'll never write
the Great Australian Novel,
laugh our way through Mills and Boon
or bodice-ripping melodramas
for the local theatre group.

The words we thought
were ours to share forever,
back and forth with time,
now slip through fingers into
dunes piled high with memory

that can't be turned again.
The tide is running out.
I watch you crawl
across that sandy sentence
sideways, slowly, towards the sea.

Croix de La Rochette

In France, the kitchen windowsill
doubled as an extension of the fridge.
Strawberries, butter and cream stood side by side
basking in the cool moist air.

For breakfast we ate walnut bread
and drank coffee in large bowls
bringing its warmth to our lips
with both hands, like a lover.

At midday on the dot we dined
on food and wine refined through years
of happy gatherings in gardens
and the market place.

When the angelus rang at seven
we gathered in the strawberries
sipped on memories of a summer's day
and knew we were in heaven.

Good Friday

I thought it was a game,
this slow progression
around the table
from chair to chair,
an endless chain of point
and counterpoint:
'I will, I won't,
I do, I don't,
never, ever, always.'

And then, one morning,
before the sun had laddered
the world with broken shafts,
that biblical cock,
the one that crows,
guided me
to the thirteenth seat.

Spring-cleaning

My guardian angel, Virgoan to the core,
looks forward to spring cleaning.
Last night she crept across my world,
sprayed leaves with an organic cleanser,
and collected orbs of dirt and dust
accumulated since last we cleaned.
I woke to sounds of nothing falling;
shards of sunlight lit up
dancing motes of dust that knew
we never would remove them,
even though their presence proved
their winter absence never was.

It's midday now and she's already
rearranged the budding vine; leaves
like tiny foreskins await erections to protect
their shadow from the burning sun
and shade the windows from its heat.
With a flick of a wing she whisks away
all winter's sloth from evergreens,
dips a feather in my pond
to test the magic of its ripples
and turns up the thermostat of the soil
so the sap is set to rise.

Before she leaves she puts out garden tools.
Determined not to exclude me from her frenzy
she always leaves the weeding to me.

North Terrace, Adelaide

It is the month of May
and the plane trees in North Terrace
are singing us in to winter
with notes left over from summer.
One by one they drop their leaves,
words that scuttle along the path,
pile up like pages from the past
that tell us tales of those whose plaques
we walk upon each day.

In their own way
these plain and unassuming trees
could stand as living memorials
to life and death and then re-birth,
the everlasting cycle
that adds depth
to the compost of history
all neatly packaged in one great boulevard,
the backbone of this city.

Springtime in Melbourne

Like butterflies from dead cocoons
unfolding leaves stretch out and yawn
then wing their way to the tree tops.
Below, the swarming traffic hums,
pigeons scatter after crumbs
on territorial cement.
A lazy wind, left over
from a winter still remembered,
skis down a distant slope, fingers
its way around sharp corners.

Tram bells toll the passing of the day.
Uniformed office workers carry
the weight of the world in laptops.
Gathered in groups, they
put spin on their importance,
weave through busy intersections,
disappear into high-rise eyries.

At night they re-emerge in Lygon Street,
flutter wings of iridescent brilliance
in the artificial vanity of neon.
On weekends all roads lead to the coliseum
where a one-eyed God flies high.
On Sunday night the week slams shut,
opens next day on a brand new page,
black ants crawling across *The Age*.

Ward Round, 1952

Every week, the routine never varies.
Trussed like a chicken, you await the chef.
Your feet, flattened by shroud-like
envelope corners begin to cramp.
Pins and needles in your bottom
stitch a patch of numbness to your body.
You dare not move, you might
rumple Sister's pride and joy,
a row of beds like coffins, so neat
you don't notice patients in them
which is why the white coats,
hovering like spectres at your feet,
speak over your head
as if you're already dead.
They see only your illness,
poke and prod and analyse it
the third person in their conversation.

After they've gone, you curl up in bed,
seek a little solitary warmth
to overcome unspoken fear.

Order in the House

With the self-importance
of a chosen few
gulls and terns fly in
opposing teams
sporting black or white.

Standing on rocky pillars
they start the day
deceptively
in silent contemplation
eagerly awaiting
the raucous interchange
of questions without notice
when, hurling insults in the air
like pieces of discarded fish
that smell of twisted truths
their words spin out,
dead as a broken promise.

Stabbed in the back
by a rival beak
the leader falls from his perch
mouthing platitudes from the floor
while a flurry of ruffled feathers
rises to the occasion
and repositions seats
in their appointed order.

Ypres, Belgium, 1950

Moon shadow from the Menin Gate,
a friendly arm across our shoulders,
guides us through a darkened square
muffled with muted memory.

The inn is warm with the quiet voice
of men who live with ghosts
they do not wish to waken;
we are joined by two young boys,
too young.
'Eenglish?' they ask
'*Mais non,*' I reply
in schoolgirl French,
'*nous sommes Australiens,*'

Points of honour move over
travel down another line
silver echo of a phantom train of thought.
'Ah!' they smile, '*Australiens*'
and we find ourselves surrounded,
entrenched by unknown friends.
'*Une bière?*' they offer
and we smile 'Yes.'

The boy who's lost an arm
asks me to dance
and so we dance
where men from both our countries
have danced to a different tune
but died in the same embrace.

In the moon dust shadow of dead men's souls
we are given the key to their castle.

Soldier Settler

In threadbare jeans of struggle
held up by a belt-strained mortgage
he battles on,
his face a reconnaissance map
of quiet desperation.

In spite of skirmishes
around the minefield of his budget,
interest rates that rise as prices fall
and unforgiving seasons
tearing at his hopes –

he still loves this place.

Like ingrained soil on leathered skin
it is as much a part of him
as dogs that shadow his mind
or galahs that punctuate
his morning thoughts
with screeching commas.

He is, they say, the salt of the earth
fighting to save the land
he would have died for once.
But in the shelter of his years
watching his sons take up the fight,
he sometimes ponders on
the paradox of pyrrhic victories.

After the War

The friends who welcomed back
their hero have all gone,
leaving these two alone
but not together.
Years of words unspoken
hang between them.

She, left behind
in dread anticipation
of the final blow,
wore the precious perfume
of his chair, his books, his clothes,
in bitter silence.

He, drowning in a living death
that haunts him still,
tied himself in knots
to keep his heart in place for her
through the lonely darkness
of nights they could not share.

Side by side they sit,
shy and embarrassed
as if just introduced.
They long to feel
but also fear
the touch of the past.

Arms Dealer

Cradled in a lover's arms
the touch of silky patina on skin
arouses him.

Satin smooth and sleek the butt
sits sweetly in his hand's desire,
fits neatly in his grand design
of victory over vanquished.
He will not turn the other cheek.
The virgin's sheet will soon
be stained with blood.

With wordy excuse
to justify his role,
he eases his conscience
into the comfortable chair
of his own rhetoric.

Cushioned into complacency
by tax-deductible donations
he gives,
with the generosity of spent bullets,
as much to one side
as to the other.

Suspect

No, he wasn't tortured.
Here, we abide by the rules
of the Geneva Convention.
He was treated
as humanely as a dog:
chained by the neck,
fed and watered every day,
exercised twice a week;
and in order
to protect him
from himself and others,
kept in isolation
for eighteen months.

Oh no, he wasn't tortured.

But for the Grace

He could have been me
but he was born
on the wrong side of the border.

He could have been me
but his hunger
was fed hollow words.

He could have been me
but the walls around him
crumbled to dust.

He could have been me
but for the roll
of a dice…

his throw landed him
in detention,
mine, outside the wire.

Enigma

Today the tide is telling tales
slipping in to the vernacular
of tongues turned loose
in ebb and flow,
gossiping around my feet.

Rumours, hasty, rash and ill-considered,
drag my footprints
through the shifting shallows,
turning inside out,
like a discarded sock,
that which once I thought I knew.

Bits of truth lie scattered
on the receding shore,
upside down or back to front,
missing pieces of a jigsaw
waiting to complete the picture.

Washed away
before I can retrieve them,
I am left with unwritten answers
to questions I did not ask.

Coming Home in Spring

From the moment the ferry docks
we smell it –
clover –
sweet and sickly.

Hanging in the air like fairy floss,
it sticks to our skin,
assails our nostrils,
blocks out all thoughts we might have had,
just by being there
and drapes our memories
with scented flowers.

Fed on sun and nightly dew
it grows like mushroom spore,
until we see lambs dancing
in our mind's eye

and we know it's September.

Evensong

In a world of muted touch
the setting sun dissolves
the far horizon
into an indigo lake.

Silhouetted,
two scribbly gums
trace love songs in the air,
their elongated shadows
entwined like lovers;

strips of bark
that once concealed
their pure white trunks
fall to the floor,
discarded clothing,

and darkness,
now descending,
drapes their nakedness
with dew.

Reveille

Every morning
our bowler-hatted magpie
struts outside my window.

With one leg tucked under his wing
like a furled umbrella,
or perhaps the *Fin Review*,
he hedges his funds,
assesses rates of exchange
and grabs crumbs from Treasury benches
to trade with interest for a song.

But oh! What a wonderful song!

Road Kill

That final leap was your best;
a sudden burst of flame
whose ultimate brilliance
extinguished itself.

Your landing leaves you
seemingly unblemished –
head on dusty pillow,
paws in fitful prayer –

but in the sadness of your eye
the heavens you sought to reach
pass by.

Fishing at Chapman River

Your cast
snaps at a patch of air
wrapping it around the line
in a sibilant sigh
that ends with a soothing plop,
releasing thoughts
from below the surface.

Dappled sunlight
dances on the water
like silver shards of fish
that are not there;

all we catch
are half-remembered tales
hanging in the branches
of the ancient paperbarks
trailing like leaves
at the water's edge.

It's not a day
for catching fish
but then we knew
it wasn't meant to be;
the pleasure's in the chase
and not the capture.

Words we never speak
hang between our laughter
and the lip that sips the wine
holding hands to form a net
for catching dreams.

I know you will be back –
you've left cockles in my freezer.

Paper Nautilus

Every seven years they come,
these gifts from the sea.
Every seven years I walk,
my ghost and I,
into the teeth of the easterlies
along the cutting edge of dawn.

This year I found my nautilus,
its cup too fine to hold my thoughts.

I look,
but dare not touch.

New Year's Eve

Penneshaw, 2000

Cradled in the dancing bay
happiness in children's voices
plaits the sky above
with threads of memory;
hangs,
like gold dust,
in the ever changing clouds.

Near by,
on basalt missiles
rising from the shore,
a chorus of a capella gulls
sings
in strident harmony
unique to first rehearsals.

Above,
a lonely albatross
hovers in the chaise longue of a thermal
studying attentively
his fish-eye world
below

where
a young man with a Pentax
tunnels vision to the far horizon,
traps one-hundredth of a second
in a time warp
between two millennia.

At the appropriate hour
when brushstrokes of a dancing light
paint the midnight velvet
with exploding flowers

the up and coming century
elbows out the old.

July in Penneshaw

It happens every winter.
Froth and foam outline a mouth
that bites into the bay with hunger,
swallowing the beach.

Rugged up, we watch in awe.
Wind whips our cheeks
cleansing us of all complacency;
flecks of foam fly by

like words from a lover's tiff,
stormy eruptions
of a hidden passion
that seethes below the surface.

Back home, we toast our feet
by the fire, sip hot soup.
Enya enfolds us in *Watermark*.
Books plead to be read.

Next day, the freshly laundered shore
flaps wet towels around our legs.
Waves breathe with the regularity
of exhausted sleep.

A sooty tern, with strands
of seaweed flying, proclaims
upon a banner of grey sky,
the season's turning.

Sea Song

Take me down to the sea with you
and I will be your lover true.

So sang the whispering wind of dawn
so sang the moon to the dying morn
wake me,

take me down to the sea with you
and I will be your lover true.

Two kestrels rode on the ocean's breast
one kestrel wept when the other left,
wake me,

take me down to the sea with you
and I will be your lover true.

To the silver bells of the sea that rang
six dolphins danced, six dolphins sang
wake me,

take me down to the sea with you
and I will be your lover true.

The tide burst open along the shore
and love cried out do not for-
sake me,

take me down to the sea with you
and I will be your lover true.

Snug Cove, Kangaroo Island

Running to keep
her rendezvous with the moon,
the ocean's swirling skirts
catch on the shallow shore,
leaving behind watery patches,
holes torn in a bridal train.
Waiting to be mended
they strip the stranded clouds
ready for the turning tide
to stitch them, invisibly,
into place.

This is a lover's beach.
Each day the sea brings in its shells
like wedding gifts
leaving behind
the grit and grain
that build the depth of love.

Treading Grapes

When your fingertips brush
the nape of my neck,
the liquid desire
of our first pressing
washes over me.

I savour this moment
like mellow wine
tended with care
by the warmth of your sun
and brought to me
from the cellar of your heart.

Delicious.

Villanelle

He came to me soft when the night was still
on a moonbeam shaft through the mist-sweet air,
and I whispered to him, I will, I will.

I'll love you forever he said, until
death tears us both from each other's care,
so come to me soft now the night is still.

Let me your maiden's dreams fulfil
with a tender kiss and love sweet-shared
and I whispered to him, I will, I will.

When silvered words from a feathered quill
shimmered like jewels in the pitch-black air,
he came to me soft when the night was still.

The message was clear, 'tis easy to kill
a love so pure, so beware, take care.
And I whispered to him, I will, I will.

Through valleys of doubt and o'er wondrous hills
on a moonbeam shaft through the mist-sweet air,
he comes to me soft when the night is still
and I whisper to him, I will, I will.

I am Orange

My lanterns float in a pool of leaves,
cut through the air with autumn's eye
and light the way to winter's solstice.
I mould the ivory wax of the moon
until it is full, delicious and ripe.
When you peel me, feel my flesh firm
to your touch. Let my juices fill
your mouth with summer madness.
In the harem of your garden I am called
Favourite. I bring the sun to your bed.

Golden Wedding

Throughout his life
the strains of Woody Herman*
dogged his footsteps
like a tenacious shadow,
dancing in and out
along the path
he trod with her,
an echo to his heart.

As records go
he kept the beat
full well.

His quickstep,
after fifty years,
still leads her
to a lover's
rumpled sheet.

*Noted drummer of the Jazz Age well-known for his *Golden Wedding*

Pruning the Vine

His days are growing shorter. Every winter,
prunes his daughter's vine. Speaks not of love
but demonstrates in silence how to curve
with care the plant that once he grafted into

ancient stock; trellis-trains the frame
of younger years, nips in the bud all wayward
shoots, removes dead wood, supplies the food
for thoughts to blossom, for fire to flame.

His summer fruit drips honey on the vine,
sweetens hours spent in dappled shade,
sings the vintage in the vat and adds
youthful effervescence to his wine.

Love, rusted onto well-worn pruning shears
grows deeper with the weathering of years.

Dried Figs

My brain is like an old fig tree,
he said, the shrivelled fruit inedible.
At least, that's what he would have said
could he have found the words;
but they had fallen, like leaves
from wintry branches,
to lie at his feet, hidden and confused,
amongst the debris of a lifetime.

And he would have added, if he could,
it's because of the drought, you see:
we haven't had a decent rain for years
and even now it would be too late,
too late for the fruit to ripen
and fall, plump with nostalgia,
into the vacant lap of the past
filled with forgotten memories.

In the Shadow of Each Other's Presence

Do you remember
how the wrinkles of your smile
folded my loneliness
into the flight of a bird?

Tucked under your wing
we dipped and soared
on a flight we neither knew
nor cared would be so chequered.

Smooth as a singing glider,
rough as a thermal landing,
your wing still wraps around me,
your touch still fills my now.

Lost

You hold me
in the pupil of your eye.
For years I've found myself
reflected there,
the I of me.

But now
the lid is closing;
shut out
I cannot find myself.

Rehearsal

They are both playing a part.

He repeats his words
because he can't help it.

She repeats hers
because she has to.

She helps him on and off the stage
adjusts his costume
prompts him from the wings
and smiles, like a pro, at the audience.

But, behind the curtains of her mind
she knows

that when he makes his final bow
her next role will be

a monologue.

Maxie

Like him
the dog is dying.
No longer can she jump for joy,
her food is left uneaten
and every day she digs her grave
just a little deeper.
The worst is that hang-dog look,
those pleading eyes,
life dripping from an open mouth
like a leaking tap.
He doesn't have that sort of washer
but he does have a bullet.
At the sound of the shot
dead leaves scatter and
her dying tail wags furiously
in a race against time to say 'thank you'.

Like her
he can't do what he used to.
Takes hours to dig the soil to bury her.
When a paw appears, he puts it from his mind
as if taking it down from his lap
before walking together into a younger world,
a winter wind planing her silken coat.
He knows he'll miss the comfort of her
sitting at his feet each night
but is glad she will no longer
be hanging in there
like him.

Cliff Edge

The path grows steep and narrow,
and the trees have shut down for winter,
their leaves scattered like
words looking for a sentence
we do not want to read.

In silence, we scuff them over the edge.

Ever the gentleman, you walk on the outside,
now undermined through age.
If you fall, I cannot save you,
but if we hold hands,
you might take me with you.

Wreckage

Far off, the lowering storm of death
devours the horizon's bridge and snaps

my anchor chain. Unhinged and cast adrift,
I try to catch the lifeline of your voice

but the deafening drum of the deep drowns
out all sound, save that of its own collapse.

Waves rise up to fall upon waves,
relentless, overpowering;

angry sickles scythe the sea,
chew up, spit out on distant shores

the indigestible remains
of vented spleen and frothing anger.

The pale blue waters of my dreams
run darker, ever darker.

Death is Never Convenient

Like an uninvited guest
death is never fully catered for.
It gate crashes our world,
reorganises the menu,
changes plans without notice,
and with its own peculiar panic
leaves us unexpectedly at a loss.

It never cleans up its own mess,
or sorts out belongings, wills or estates.
And to make matters worse,
it always arrives either early or late,
never, ever, dead on time.

Insomnia

Last night insomnia sat
for a chat on my bed.
Handcuffed to the moon
he came through the window
on a band of light as broad as day,
as long as a sleepless night,
tossed me from side to side
like a hollow log
and would not go away.

I thought he might leave
if I made him a cup of tea,
but he sat on my shoulder,
drank the pot dry and talked
so much I returned to bed
just to get him off my back.
Yet still he stayed
till sun broke down the dawn.

I never slept. It was, I think,
the timbre of his voice,
the familiar touch of his words
that seeped under my skin
and pleaded to be heard.

You see, he could have been you.

Alone

I want to touch you
but my hands are tied.

I want to hear you
but you're not there.

I want to sing you
but the music's died.

I want to smell you
but the bloom is bare.

I want to see you
but the glass is dark.

I want to feel you
but I can't, I can't.

Love Letters

In the alphabet of love
they both chose the letter C.
When they met, blindly,
they snapped together like magnets,
aware they had found
what they didn't know
they were looking for.

Like two parallel beams
they gave each other strength,
overcame weakness,
steady and steadfast.

At night they curled together,
his hand resting lightly on her hip
or cupping a breast.
When one turned over
the other followed,
as if hinged together.

When one half of the hinge
rusted and broke off
she took the two Cs
and turned them into an O,
wherein to hide her grief.

Orpheus and Eurydice

He
could not feel her eyes
upon his back,
so he turned.

She,
with wings of grace
brushing against desire,
reached towards
his backward glance
but slipped and fell
into a bowl of stars
where words do not exist.

Curve of her cheek
still lies between
the sickle moon
and a young man's dream.

Last Words

for my father

I love you, I said.

The man, the bed,
a mound of snow,
fragile flakes
waiting to melt.

Wintry winds
seeped through the opening door
icy fingers
a vice around my heart.

I took the hand
that held the steering wheel for me,
felt it change down a gear or two
readying for the home run.

Cradled in mine
like a newborn child,
I pressed it to my lips,
a bridge between us.

I love you, I said.

Then the snow melted.

www.ingramcontent.com/pod-product-compliance
Lightning Source LLC
Chambersburg PA
CBHW070917080526
44589CB00013B/1331